THE WILD WORLD OF ANIMALS

THE WILD WORLD OF ANIMALS

PENGUINS

MARY HOFF

CREATIVE EDUCATION

Special thanks to Dr. Tony Williams, Simon Fraser University, and to Natasha Williams.

Published by Creative Education, 123 South Broad Street, Mankato, Minnesota 56001. Creative Education is an imprint of The Creative Company. Designed by Rita Marshall. Production design by Advertising & Design, Inc. Photographs by Alamy (Bruce Coleman Brakefield, Bryan and Cherry Alexander Photography, Danita Delimont, Robert Fried, Martin Harvey, Mike Hill, ImageState, INFOCUS Photos, NORMA JOSEPH, kris mercer, Natural Visions, Robert Slade, Steve Bloom Images, Maximilian Weinzierl), Getty Images (Frans Lemmens, Joseph Van Os, Art Wolfe).

Library of Congress Cataloging-in-Publication Data: Hoff, Mary King. Penguins / by Mary Hoff. p. cm. — (The wild world of animals). Includes bibliographical references. ISBN-13: 978-1-58341-435-4. 1. Penguins—Juvenile literature. I. Title. II. Wild world of animals (Creative Education). QL696.S473H62 2006 598.47—dc22 2005048229.
First edition 9 8 7 6 5 4 3 2 1

It's a sunny November morning on Cape Adare, a rocky stretch of land on the coast of Antarctica. An Adélie penguin sits on a nest of pebbles, hugging two large eggs to a warm patch of skin on the bottom of its belly. All around, as far as the eye can see, thousands of other penguins are doing the same thing. Suddenly, the penguin feels a tapping beneath it. One of the chicks is chipping its way out of its shell. After a while, the chick emerges, wet and tired. The penguin shelters it as it dries into a fluffy, gray ball of **down**.

An Adélie penguin's fat keeps its eggs warm   **5**

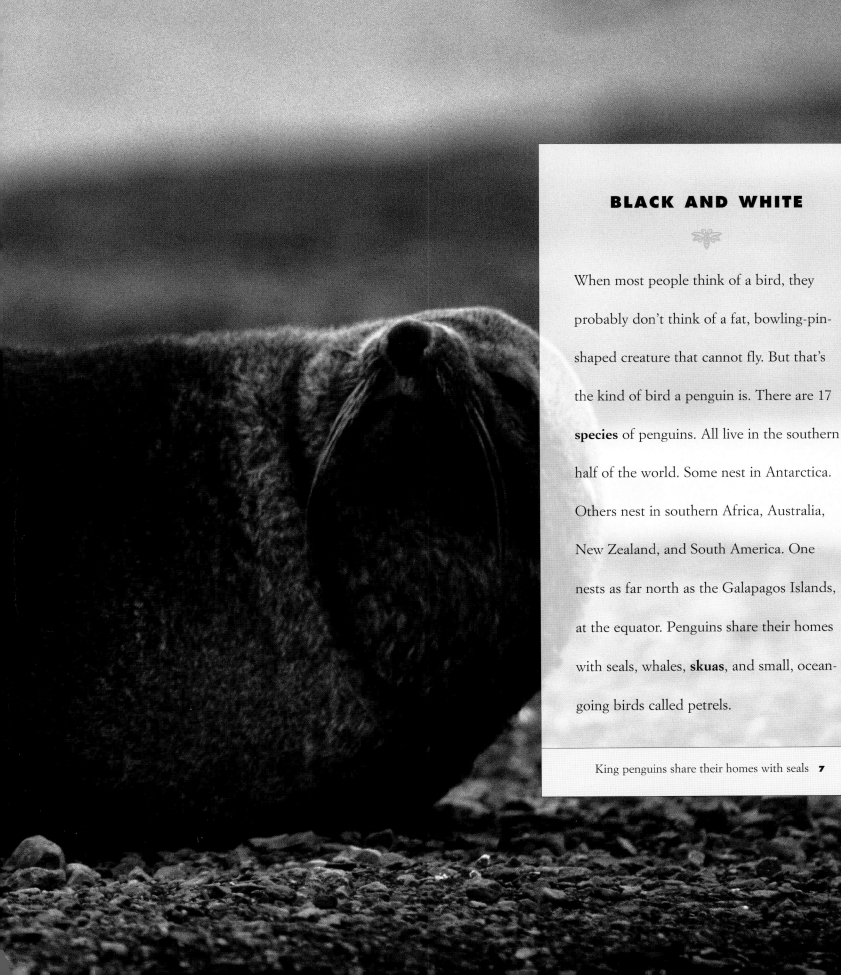

BLACK AND WHITE

When most people think of a bird, they probably don't think of a fat, bowling-pin-shaped creature that cannot fly. But that's the kind of bird a penguin is. There are 17 **species** of penguins. All live in the southern half of the world. Some nest in Antarctica. Others nest in southern Africa, Australia, New Zealand, and South America. One nests as far north as the Galapagos Islands, at the equator. Penguins share their homes with seals, whales, **skuas**, and small, ocean-going birds called petrels.

King penguins share their homes with seals **7**

Penguins have a dark back and a light-colored belly. Some also have orange or yellow markings or feathers on their head. The Adélie penguin, the species most people think of when they think of penguins, has a black head and back and a white stomach.

Adélie penguins' coloration looks like a tuxedo

The smallest penguin, the little blue penguin of Australia and New Zealand, is about 16 inches (41 cm) tall. It weighs only about two pounds (0.9 kg). The largest, the emperor penguin of Antarctica, can be close to 4 feet (1.2 m) tall and weigh 60 to 90 pounds (27–41 kg).

Little blue penguins are also called fairy penguins **9**

Penguins swim in the ocean rather than fly through the air. They have many **adaptations** that help them survive at sea. Their long, fish-shaped body moves smoothly through the water. Their heavy bones help weigh them down so they can swim underwater. Their webbed feet help them steer. When they swim, they flap their flippers like other birds flap their wings when they fly.

Many penguins can swim fast and far **11**

Penguins have thick layers of fat and special feathers that **insulate** them from cold water and air and shield them from wind. Sometimes penguins get too hot when they are on land. If they do, they fluff out their feathers and hold their flippers in the air. This helps them cool down.

Penguins can stay warm even in frozen lands　**13**

Penguins eat mainly fish, **krill**, and other ocean-going animals such as squid. Fish-eating penguins have a long, thin bill. Those that eat mainly krill have a shorter bill. A penguin's tongue and the roof of its mouth have tiny spines that help it hold on to and swallow its food.

If people drank only seawater, they would die of thirst because it's so salty. But a penguin can quench its thirst with seawater. That's because it has a gland over each eye that collects salt and removes it from its body.

Penguins swallow fish whole while swimming

LIFE AS A PENGUIN

Penguins spend much of their lives swimming and finding food at sea. They swim underwater, occasionally leaping above the surface to catch a breath of air. Most penguins can hold their breath for several minutes, and some can hold their breath for up to 20 minutes at a time. As they search for food, penguins try to avoid becoming a meal for other animals. Leopard seals, sea lions, killer whales, and sharks all have a taste for penguins.

Swimming together can help keep enemies away   **17**

When it's time to lay eggs, penguins come to shore. They waddle as they make their way from the ocean to their nesting grounds. Some toboggan, sliding across the ice and snow on their belly, to get from one place to another. Penguins may stay on land for many months. They live off of the energy in the fat they built up while they were feasting out at sea.

Some penguins walk miles to nesting grounds   **19**

Most penguins breed in the spring or summer. They gather in large groups called rookeries to mate, lay their eggs, and raise their chicks. A single rookery may have hundreds or thousands of penguins. Penguins often mate with the same partner every year.

After mating, most penguin females lay two eggs in a nest. Then they go out to sea for food. The males **incubate** the eggs while the females are away. After days or weeks, depending on the species, the female penguin returns, and the male leaves to get food. They take turns caring for the eggs.

20 Adélie penguins make their nests out of rocks

Most penguin eggs hatch about five weeks after they are laid. The chicks are covered with fluffy down. At first, the chicks stay close to their parents, who keep them warm and protect them from **predators** such as skuas. When they are several weeks old, the young of many species gather in groups called crèches. Gathering helps keep them warm and safe. Their parents bring food to them, each recognizing its own young by its cry, as human parents might recognize their children's voices.

After about eight weeks, the chicks grow adult feathers. They are now ready to swim and catch their own food.

After they have raised their young, many penguins molt, or lose their old, worn-out feathers and replace them with new ones. Penguins do not go in the water while they are molting.

King penguin chicks huddle together for warmth **23**

PENGUINS AND PEOPLE

❦

Since ancient times, penguins have been a part of the lives of people in the far southern half of the world. More than 2,000 years ago, Inca Indians harvested penguin **guano** to use as fertilizer for their crops. Natives of Tierra del Fuego, at the southern tip of South America, ate penguins and used their skin to make clothing. Australian **Aborigines** ate penguins and their eggs, too.

24   Magellanic penguins on a beach in Tierra del Fuego

The first people from the northern part of the world to see penguins most likely were explorers from Europe about 500 years ago. In 1497, Portuguese explorer Vasco da Gama's crew reported seeing flightless birds in southern Africa. On their trip around the world, Spanish explorer Ferdinand Magellan's crew saw penguins off the coast of South America.

Magellanic penguins are named after Magellan **25**

Whalers, or people who made a living by capturing whales, and explorers in search of the South Pole sometimes used penguins for food. Some whalers collected penguins and used their fat for fuel. When explorer Ernest Shackleton and his crew were stranded on Antarctic ice in the early 1900s, they survived by eating penguins and using penguin fat to fuel their stoves.

Early explorers killed up to 3,000 penguins a day   **27**

In the 1800s and early 1900s, people who

lived in the southern half of the world used

penguin oil for fuel, too. They also used

penguin skin to make purses and hats and

penguin feathers for decorations. In Africa,

people harvested penguin eggs and sold

them like grocery stores sell chicken eggs.

Today, penguins are popular animals at zoos and in cartoons and stories. Many people think they are cute because they look like little men in fancy suits. A professional hockey team is named the Pittsburgh Penguins.

Penguins have always been a favorite zoo animal **29**

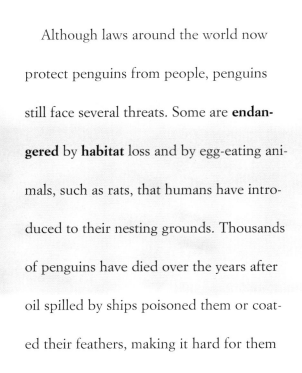

Although laws around the world now protect penguins from people, penguins still face several threats. Some are **endangered** by **habitat** loss and by egg-eating animals, such as rats, that humans have introduced to their nesting grounds. Thousands of penguins have died over the years after oil spilled by ships poisoned them or coated their feathers, making it hard for them

30 People are no longer allowed to hunt penguins

to stay warm. Some penguins are disturbed when tourists come to see them. Many people are concerned that global warming, a change in Earth's climate caused by pollution, will hurt penguins' food supply and destroy their habitat. Fortunately, many scientists are working to protect penguins. With their help, these beautiful and unusual birds will continue to thrive in the wild.

In some places, penguin numbers are on the rise **31**

GLOSSARY

Aborigines are dark-skinned, native people of Australia.

Adaptations are features of a living thing that help it survive where it lives.

Down is the name for the fluffy feathers that cover some baby birds.

An **endangered** animal is one that is at risk of dying off so that it no longer exists on Earth.

Guano is another name for the droppings of sea birds or bats.

The place where a creature lives is called its **habitat**.

When birds **incubate** their eggs, they keep them warm so the new bird inside can grow.

When things **insulate** an animal, they protect the animal from heat or cold.

Krill are small, ocean-going animals that look like shrimp.

Predators are animals that kill and eat other animals.

Skuas are duck-sized seabirds that eat penguin eggs and chicks and other living things.

Some animals are divided into different kinds, or **species**. Members of a species can have young together.

BOOKS

Magloff, Lisa. *Watch Me Grow: Penguin.* New York: DK Publishing, 2004.

Schlein, Miriam. *What's a Penguin Doing in a Place Like This?* Brookfield, Conn.: The Millbrook Press, 1997.

Zoehfeld, Kathleen Weidner. *Penguins.* New York: Scholastic, 2002.

WEB SITES

KidZone Penguins http://www.kidzone.ws/animals/penguins

National Geographic.com Kids http://www.nationalgeographic.com/kids/creature_feature/0101/penguins.html

Penguins Around the World http://www.siec.k12.in.us/~west/proj/penguins

INDEX